50
88

Youth talks
with God

YOUTH
TALKS WITH GOD

A Book
of
Everyday
Prayers

by Avery Brooke

CHARLES SCRIBNER'S SONS

NEW YORK

PREFACE

THIS is a book of prayers written in plain words and about everyday things.

Prayers, after all, are not meant to be said just in church, or in a special language. They should be woven into our daily life and be as natural to us as our conversations with our friends. But unlike our friends, God can see inside us and know whether we mean what we say. What really matters when we are talking to God is not what we say with our lips but what we mean in our hearts.

However, it is often hard to put into words what we have in our hearts. This is why prayers have been written —to help us say what we cannot always find words to express in our own way.

Some prayers have spoken so well for all men that they have been used for hundreds of years. But, prayers which are said for hundreds of years are not in the words that we use in talking to each other today. Even some of the new prayers that we may hear or read have old-fashioned ways of saying things and often these prayers seem to have nothing to do with us.

Words have sometimes been called "the clothes of prayer." But often the clothes of a prayer hide the real prayer for us. They may be beautiful words, but because we don't understand everything they mean, we have a hard time seeing the prayer behind them.

And yet prayers in old words, new words, or our own words can be very much the same underneath the clothes. The prayers in this book have been written in the hope that it will be easy to discover the prayers behind the words and through them, find more meaning in all prayer.

A. B.

NOTE

Please note that in the prayers when *he* appears one may substitute *she* or the name of a specific person. In one or two places a blank has been left in which the name of the particular person in mind can be inserted.

Contents

9

A Morning Prayer

O GOD, stay with me through this day. Fill my heart with love for thee and everyone I meet.

If someone is sad, help me to comfort *him*.

If someone is unfair, help me to forgive *him*.

If someone is angry, help me to be patient with *him*.

If someone especially needs love, help me to love *him*.

And when things go wrong today, O God, let me remember to ask thy help.

Whether People Like Me

 GOD, help me to remember that what is really important is not whether people like me but whether I like people.

Help me to search out the good things in people, the things to like them for, and help me to forget the bad things. But most of all, help me not to mind when my feelings are hurt, but to care a lot when other people's feelings are hurt.

To Try

O FATHER, help me to know what it means to try, to try very hard and sometimes to fail and to try again. Help me to try to do the new thing, and the things I think too hard for me. Then when I try and fail, help me to be cheerful and not afraid but ready to try again. Amen

13

When Someone Has Been Unfair

OD, someone has been unfair to me. I did what I should have done and *he* didn't and no one cares.

I want very much to do something, but there is nothing I can do and inside I feel angry and hurt.

O God, please calm my heart and give me the strength to accept cheerfully what I cannot change.

When I Want
to Do Something Wrong

O GOD, I want to do something I know is wrong. Please help me not to do it. Show me all the reasons why I shouldn't and give me strength to stand by them. Fill my heart with so much love for thee that I want to please thee more than I want to please myself.

Learning

LORD, I thank thee for the excitement of learning something new.

I thank thee for the chance to learn what things are made of and what makes them work, for the beauty felt in someone's heart and made real to me in words, in music and in art, and for the men of past times I read about who dreamt, and dared, and did great things that changed the world.

But, Lord, there are times when there is no excitement in it, when learning is all dull and endless work. Help me then, Lord. Teach me to be patient, to work hard and long when I must and to play later. Remind me of the good feeling of a hard job well done and of the new adventures that open when a skill is learned. And help me, Lord, as I learn, to see not only man's hand in all the wonders of the earth but thine.

Not to Be Too Proud

O LORD, when I know I am better than my friends at doing something, it seems stupid to pretend I'm not. But help me, Lord, not to be too proud. Quiet my tongue when I would boast. Help me not to hurt the feelings of the person less good at it than I. Remind me how the loser feels so I can know what to say or do to make *him* feel better.

When Very Happy

O LORD, when we are brimful of happiness and our hearts leap at the goodness of life, then help us to share this joy with the world. Let us not be misers, counting our happiness in solitude but use it as freely as thou hast given it to us. Help us to use it by praying for those less happy than we, by quickened love and understanding for those we daily see, and by active rememberance of those we seldom see.

A Prayer for Someone Very Sick

O GOD, _____ is very sick. I know *he* is in pain and maybe *he* will even die. O God, if there is anything I can do to show *him* that I love *him,* help me to do it.

O God, thou who made *him* and all creation and who desirest not the pain of thy children, bring *him* joy and health once more, that *he* may live and serve thee in gladness and love.

Someone Having Trouble

O JESUS, if I see someone having trouble, help me to stop instead of walking by. Help me to feel *his* trouble as if it were my own. Tell me what to say or do to make it right and to feel love for *him* in *his* trouble, when *he* most needs love.

To See A Lot of People

GOD, I'm going to see a lot of people and I'm afraid I'll be wearing the wrong clothes, say the wrong thing and act the wrong way. I'm afraid no one will like me, and way down deep I'm afraid someone will laugh at me.

Help me, God! Take away my fear. I know it is stupid and still I'm afraid. Help me to know that other people are really afraid too and that behind smiling faces they feel cold and alone. Help me to want to soothe their fears and make them happy.

Help me to think of them and forget myself.

To Pray
for Someone Else

O GOD, teach me to pray for someone other than myself; for the sick and poor and hungry, for people who are unhappy and people who are afraid. Help me to feel their problems as if they were my own, so that I may pray for them not just with words but with my heart.

For Prisoners
in Far Countries

GOD, if sometimes I cannot do as I want and it makes me angry, help me to remember the thousands who can never do what they want, who are hungry and cold and afraid and far away from home.

O God, let them know thee and give them hope in their misery and, if it be possible, give them freedom once again.

To Be Patient with
My Mother and Father

GOD, help me to be patient with my mother and father. Help me to forgive them when they lose their tempers or are unfair or when they just don't listen. Help me to know that sometimes even when they try to understand, they don't.

Help them to understand me, God, and help me to understand them, so that together we may come closer to thee.

The World Is Before Me

O CHRIST, I am young and the world is before me and I could do many things. Help me to choose wisely where I should go and what I should do. Help me to see where I may serve thee best. Let me see what my talents are and what is merely pride or dreams. And O Christ, let me never follow a path that leads away from thee!

When I Have Lost Myself

O GOD, I thank you for the place where no one goes but you and I; for the secret field, the tree, the rock, the corner in the house, where I may go and find myself again and in finding me, find you.

What longed-for peace creeps in upon my heart, when, hidden in this secret place, I listen to the silence and slowly lose that tightness that held me fast, unhappy and afraid!

In time I find I can look around at your quiet things, the leaf so very near my head, the lines on the board beneath my feet or the bird that scolds a bit because I'm here and flies away. And when I've looked at those awhile and rested in the hush, I know that you are near and I can find myself again.

Good and Bad Fortune

GOD, help me to be thankful for all the good things in my life and not take them for granted. And when things go wrong, help me not to be too sorry for myself, but to remember so many other people whose life is much harder: people who are always a little hungry, who are sick with no one to care for them, who have ability but no chance to learn. Help me to pray for them and forget myself.

For Teachers

O LORD, I pray for teachers, not only my own but everyone's.

Help them when their pupils don't want to learn. Comfort them when their hours are too long and no one thinks so. Strengthen them when their work is dull but must be done.

Grant, O Lord, that they may really understand what they are trying to teach and know how to tell us what they understand. And above all, give both to all teachers and to all students a great patience and a great love, that we may give our best to each other.

The Test

O LORD, I haven't used my eyes, my ears or my mind the way you would have me. Now it is too late. I know I can't ask you to put facts in my head I should have put there long ago, but, O Lord, help me not to forget what I have learned and not to be so tense I do not do my best.

And when the test is over, let me remember to use all my chances to learn and not again waste them because I am lazy or thoughtless.

Wonder and Joy

O LORD, when I hold a budding twig in my hand and wonder at it or see with joy the sky, sunswept and clean after night, help me to remember that they are thy creation, and in remembering, come closer to thee.

When Someone Has Died

O CHRIST,_____whom
I loved very much has died and there is an
empty place I cannot fill. My heart aches and
all inside I feel stiff and tired.

Help me, Christ, to look straight at that empty
place and not be frightened. Help me to be glad for
him because *he* is happy with thee. And, O God, help
me to be unafraid to walk the earth without *him* but
to take strength and comfort from thy love.

For Peace

O CHRIST, teach us the ways of peace so that when we come to manhood we may practice them.

Teach us to understand the strange customs of other lands and to love the people from countries that are afraid of and hate us. Teach us not to boast that our country is best, even though we love her. Teach us to be ready to give up some of our comforts and power and pride, so that war will leave the face of the earth and we may work for thee in peace.

For Leaders

O GOD, help our leaders to lead. Whether they are friends our age whom everyone copies or kings and presidents, help them to use their power well. Don't let them get so proud they forget what they are doing or so busy that they forget thee. Fill them with so much love that they can understand their followers and make peace with their enemies.

In Thanks

O LORD, I thank thee for the sky and sea and air, for all the places I know and love and places I have not yet seen but may in time to come.

I thank thee for my friends and family and for the people I know who teach thy love to me by their example. I thank thee for the chance to learn and grow and change. I thank thee for loving me even when I fail thee and for always letting me try again.

Hate

O FATHER, when I would hate someone who has hurt me, or whose ways are not my ways, change my heart. Root out my bitterness and give me of thy love that I may understand *him* and me, deeply and truly, and know why *he* is as *he* is and why I am as I am.

I Am Very Sorry

O GOD, I am very sorry that I did what I did. I knew it wasn't right and yet I couldn't help it. I know now God, if I had thought of you and asked your help, you would have helped me. Forgive me, God, and help me to remember you always.

Bewildered

O LORD, when I am bewildered and the world is all noise and confusion around me and I don't know which way to go and am frightened, then be thou with me. Put thy hand on my shoulder and let thy strength invade my weakness and thy light burn the mist from my mind. Help me to step forward with faith in the way I should go.

God Make Me Well

O GOD, I have been sick a long time and almost forgotten how it feels to be well. The doctors do their best but they take a very long time. Help me to be as cheerful as I can so that my family are not too unhappy.

And, O God, please make me well, so that my body can feel full of joy and I can run and shout and work and get tired and sleep and wake up happy.

When Angry
with A Friend

O FATHER, I am very angry with my friend and I don't want to be. Help me to calm my anger before I say or do the wrong thing. Show me why *he* acted the way *he* did and let me understand *him*.

If I did something wrong, help me to know it and say I'm sorry. If I did nothing wrong, help me to be patient and forgive *him*.

In Thanks for Happy Times

O LORD, I thank thee that I am alive, that my eyes can see and my ears can hear and my heart can feel. I thank thee for the early sunshine on a new day, when I feel strong and wonder what the day will bring. I thank thee for the sparkling hours that come sometimes without warning when everything is suddenly very real and friends seem really friends and every pebble in the road and every leaf on every tree has being and so do I.

I thank thee too for quieter times, when in warm and silent sun I sit and think and wander in my mind through past and present and what I wish to do, and in the quietness my mind grows clear and my heart sees the paths that I should walk and holds them dear.

Afraid to Be Found Out

O LORD, I have done something wrong and I am afraid I will be found out. I am ashamed, but more than that, I am afraid that people who love me will be ashamed.

O Lord, I know it is my fault that I have done this thing and it cannot be undone but help me not to be a coward. If I ought to confess to someone, give me the courage. If I can make things better, show me how. And above all, do not let me add bad to bad because I am too afraid to let someone know what I have done.

The End of A Bad Day

O FATHER, I hurt inside tonight. Nothing has gone the way it should. I didn't do very well and people thought I did worse than I did. Take the tiredness away from me, God; make me feel all in one piece again. Show me what I should do to make things better. Then let thy peace descend on my heart so I can sleep well and get up tomorrow with thy happiness upon me and ready to do better.

God's Workers

GOD, help thy own workers, those who spend their lives not only trying to follow thee but helping others find thee.

Help the ministers and the teachers and the secretaries and the missionaries. Help the men who must be in charge of many men.

Do not let them lose sight of thee because they have too much to do, but give them a dream of what they might do and thy love and patience to do it.

For Old People

O LORD, help the old, and help me to be good to them.

Help me to love and understand them and know that their feelings get hurt just as mine do, and that they too sometimes get tired and cross.

Help them too in their own problems, like being alone so much, and not being as strong as they used to be. Give them strength when they are not feeling well and courage when they are sometimes afraid of tomorrow.

Little Things

LORD, help me with the little things that I forget. Remind me of the compliment that I should give, the letter to the friend I miss, the kind word I meant to speak to someone sad.

And when there are little things I want to do but shouldn't, hold me back. Help me to stop the cutting word, the boast, the scorn, the unkind laugh.

In all these things, O Lord, help me to remember always how the other person feels and to act in love towards *him*.

Friendship

O GOD, I thank thee for my friends and all the joys that they have brought. I thank thee for the happiness of sharing work and problems and laughter, and for the joy of adventuring and learning together. I thank thee for the chance to love and be loved, not because of cleverness or goodness but in spite of faults and differences.

For the Hungry
and Hopeless

O LORD, in many places that I have not seen there are people hungry and without hope. Sometimes because I am not near them I forget and because I have not felt their troubles they don't seem real. But when I stop and dare to think, I know that they are real.

O Lord, help these people that I do not know, and help me to help them. Give them strength and hope and take away their despair.

Doubt

GOD, when all the world looks grey and dirt shows everywhere and nothing is as it should be, I wonder if you really are.

O God, help me when I feel like this! Help me to remember the days when you were near and I knew it. Even when you seem far away, help me never to turn my back on you. Set me on the path to you and help me hold fast through the night, until I find your light once more.

For Those in Pain

O GOD, when I in happy health can run and breathe and sleep without thinking it might be otherwise, do not let me forget those for whom each step is a fight with pain.

O God, help them! Make the unbearable, bearable and soften the constant hurt. Give them hope for the future, and courage for the present, and comfort from knowing thee.

The Way I Look

O GOD, when I worry that people will not like the way I look, or speak, or act—help me to remember that they look at me a lot less than I think, but that you watch me always.

A Blessing

O LORD, bless all the people that I love, at home, in school and far away. Guide them by night and by day and keep them always under thy loving care.

And, O Lord, bless too the people that I don't love as I should. Teach me to understand them and love them in spite of their faults. Help me to forgive those who act badly towards me and especially bless them as they need my love and thine.

A Nightly Prayer

O FATHER, stay close to me while I sleep and all tomorrow. When I am afraid, give me strength. When I am angry, make me patient. When I think only of myself, make me remember others. When I would be unkind, let me be stopped by thoughts of thee.

And, O Father, when someone needs my love, show me how to love them.

In Thanksgiving for
Thy Church

O CHRIST, I thank thee that I am never alone in trying to follow thee. Across the world today and yesterday and in eternity I have great company. When I try, there are those who try also; when I fail, there are those who fail too; when I am forgiven, I am never alone; when my heart sings thy praises, I sing together with thy saints.

How Large Is Thy Love!

O LORD, how large is thy love! My heart sings to thee and the stones beneath my feet and the sky above my head sing also. All around me is thy world and I know that thou knowest all of it and it knows thy love.

My thoughts leap at the wonder of it! It is all thine, from the little stones at my feet to the unending sky above.

O Lord, such a great knowing thou hast beyond counting and such a great loving beyond measure! And I am caught up in it and sing of it to the world and to thee.

Index

DEALING WITH PEOPLE

DEALING WITH MYSELF